# THEMATIC UNIT
# WEATHER

*Written by Diane Williams*

**Teacher Created Materials, Inc.**
6421 Industry Way
Westminster, CA 92683
www.teachercreated.com

©1991 Teacher Created Materials, Inc
Reprinted, 2000

Made in U.S.A.

**ISBN-1-55734-273-3**

**Illustrated by**
*Sue Fullam and
Keith Vasconcelles*

# Table of Contents

# Introduction

*Weather* is a captivating, balanced-approach, thematic unit. Its 80 exciting reproducible pages are filled with a wide variety of lesson ideas designed for use with primary children. At its core are two high-quality children's literature selections—*Cloudy with a Chance of Meatballs* and *The Cloud Book*. For these books activities are included that set the stage for reading, encourage the enjoyment of the book, and extend the concepts gained. In addition, the theme is connected to the curriculum with activities in language arts (including daily writing suggestions), math, science, social studies, art, music, and life skills (e.g., cooking, physical education, career awareness). Many of these activities encourage cooperative learning. Suggestions and patterns for bulletin boards and unit management tools are additional time savers for the busy teacher. Furthermore, directions for student-created Big Books and a culminating activity that leads students to synthesize their knowledge in projects that can be shared beyond the classroom, highlight this very complete teacher resource.

This thematic unit includes the following:

❑ **literature selections**—summaries of two children's books with related lessons (complete with reproducible pages) that cross the curriculum

❑ **poetry**—suggested selections and lessons enabling students to write and publish their own works

❑ **planning guides**—suggestions for sequencing lessons each day of the unit

❑ **writing ideas**—daily suggestions as well as writing activities across the curriculum, including Big Books

❑ **bulletin board ideas**—suggestions and plans for student-created and/or interactive bulletin boards

❑ **homework suggestions**—extending the unit to the child's home

❑ **curriculum connections**—in language arts, math, science, social studies, art, music, and life skills such as cooking, physical education, and career awareness

❑ **group projects**—to foster cooperative learning

❑ **a culminating activity**—which requires students to synthesize their learning for a project or activity that can be shared with others

❑ **a bibliography**—suggesting additional literature and nonfiction books on the theme

---

To keep this valuable resource intact so that it can be used year after year, you may wish to punch holes in the pages and store them in a three-ring binder.

---

# Introduction *(cont.)*

## Why a Balanced Approach?

The strength of a whole-language approach is that it involves children in using all modes of communication—reading, writing, listening, illustrating, and doing. Communication skills are interconnected and integrated into lessons that emphasize the whole of language. Balancing this approach is our knowledge that every whole—including individual words—is composed of parts, and directed study of those parts can help a student to master the whole. Experience and research tell us that regular attention to phonics, other word-attack skills, spelling, etc., develops reading mastery, thereby fulfilling the unity of the whole-language experience. The child is thus led to read, write, spell, speak, and listen confidently in response to a literature experience introduced by the teacher. In these ways, language skills grow rapidly, stimulated by direct practice, involvement, and interest in the topic at hand.

## Why Thematic Planning?

One very useful tool for implementing a balanced language program is thematic planning. By choosing a theme with correlating literature selections for a unit of study, a teacher can plan activities throughout the day that lead to a cohesive, in-depth study of the topic. Students will be practicing and applying their skills in meaningful contexts. Consequently, they will tend to learn and retain more. Both teachers and students will be freed from a day that is broken into unrelated segments of isolated drill and practice.

## Why Cooperative Learning?

Besides academic skills and content, students need to learn social skills. This area of development cannot be taken for granted. Students must learn to work cooperatively in groups in order to function well in modern society. Group activities should be a regular part of school life, and teachers should consciously include social objectives as well as academic objectives in their planning. For example, a group working together to write a report may need to select a leader. The teacher should make clear to the students the characteristics of good leader-follower group interaction and monitor those characteristics just as he or she would monitor the academic goals of a project.

## Why Big Books?

An excellent cooperative, balanced-approach activity is the production of Big Books. Groups of students or the whole class can apply their language skills, content knowledge, and creativity to produce a Big Book that can become a part of the classroom library to be read and reread. These books make excellent culminating projects for sharing beyond the classroom with parents, librarians, other classes, etc. Big Books can be produced in many ways, and this thematic unit book includes directions for at least one method you may choose.

# Cloudy with a Chance of Mealballs

*by Judi Barrett*

## Summary

*A flying pancake inspires Grandpa to tell the best tall tale ever. In a town called Chewandswallow the sky delivers breakfast, lunch, and dinner. It rains soup, snows mashed potatoes, and storms hamburger! What a wonderful, tasty life, until something terrible happens.*

*Weather conditions worsen, causing food of incredible sizes and strange combinations to endanger the helpless citizens. A syrup flood, salt and pepper winds, and a tomato tornado make it necessary to flee the country.*

*Boarding boats made of peanut butter and stale bread, the townspeople sail away to a new land. How they adapt to grocery stores and refrigerators is left to the reader's imagination.*

The outline below is a suggested plan for using the various activities that are presented in this unit. You should adapt these ideas to fit your own classroom situation.

## Sample Plan

### Day 1

- Tell tall tales.
- Read *Cloudy with a Chance of Meatballs*.
- Have students retell the story.
- Do Writing Tall Tales. (page 8)
- Share stories.
- Use senses to explore food.
- Sing some weather songs. (page 58)
- After It Rains. (page 10)
- Play North, South, East, West game. (page 12)

### Day 2

- Review the story.
- Discuss a critical thinking topic. (page 6)
- Introduce Amazing Weather Facts. (page 26)
- Play Pass the Hamburger. (page 12)
- Write Rain Poems. (page 21)
- Begin model building. (page 7)

### Day 3

- Complete Food Forecasting. (page 11)
- Continue Amazing Weather Facts. (page 26)
- Complete an Adventure Story Starter. (page 9)
- Illustrate and share adventure story.
- Listen to and sing "Eat It Up!" (see bibliography, page 80)
- Write weather songs. (page 58)
- Read *Flash, Crash, Rumble, and Roll* by Franklyn M. Branley.
- Play Toss the Salad! (page 12)
- Finish building model.

# Overview of Activities

## SETTING THE STAGE

1. **Circle Time**—Sit in a big circle and tell tall tales. Start the children off with one sentence such as "The sun was shining so high in the sky that . . ." Encourage them to be really imaginative. Have fun!

2. Share tall tales, such as those about Pecos Bill or Paul Bunyan. Do the activity on page 8.

## ENJOYING THE BOOK

1. **Read**—*Cloudy with a Chance of Meatballs* for enjoyment. Sit in a cozy place and laugh together.

2. **Critical Thinking**—Talk about the book from an environmental point of view. Evaluate the ways in which the people cleaned up the mess the food created. Discuss the assets and disadvantages of food from the sky.

3. **Creative Problem Solving**—Ask the children some of the following questions: What would you do with the extra food? How could you get the pancake off the school? How would you get out of town? Allow the students to share their answers.

4. **Act**—Draw how the street looked at mealtime in the town of Chewandswallow. (page 10)

5. **Retell the story**—Draw or paint illustrations of your favorite parts.

## EXTENDING THE STORY

1. Begin Amazing Weather Facts (page 26). Continue throughout the weather unit.

2. Choose one of the story starters on page 9 and have students write a story to share with the class.

3. Read and write your own rain poems. (page 21)

4. **Physical Activities**—Play some of the activities and games on page 12.

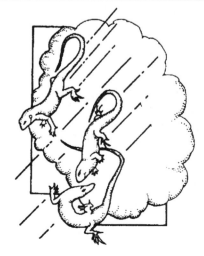

6

# Overview of Activities *(cont.)*

| EXTENDING THE STORY *(cont.)* |
| :---: |

5. Use various foods to create art projects. For collages, glue dried beans, peas, and cereals onto cardboard. Use dried pasta to create noodle art. Paint pasta of various shapes and sizes. String them to make necklaces and bracelets. Finger-paint using instant puddings of various flavors.

6. **Model Building**—Use stale bread, graham crackers, cereal, and pretzels. Use glue or peanut butter to build a house. Use broccoli or celery stalks as trees. Attach to cardboard using glue or clay. Houses can be assembled to form a city and displayed for a day.

7. **Cooking**—Cook pancakes one morning and feast! Make cream cheese and jelly sandwiches for lunch one day. Complete the "Let's Cook With Snow" activity on page 59.

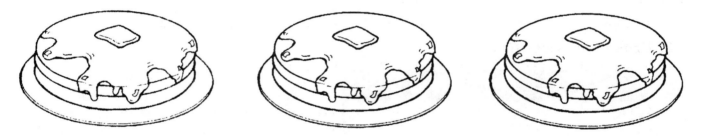

8. Evaluate the nutritional value of the meals the people had to eat in Chewandswallow. Do Food Forecasting (page 11).

9. Collect various samples of foods. Hide them in a lunch bag or use blindfolds. Ask the children to identify the foods by smell alone.

10. Sing "Eat It Up" or other food or weather songs. See bibliography (page 80) for other sources of music.

11. **Culminating Activity**—Ask the children to write their own Tall Tale book. Encourage them to divide their story into several pages and illustrate each page. Have them make a cover and print the author, illustrator, publisher and date of publication on it. Share the books with another class. Display them in the class and school libraries. Send the books home in a special envelope as a gift for the family.

# Writing Tall Tales

A tall tale is a story based on fact, but told in a highly exaggerated and humorous way. Define exaggeration for your class as something that goes beyond the truth. Explain that *Cloudy with a Chance of Meatballs* is a tall tale. How does it "go beyond the truth?" Have students discuss what makes this a tall tale (the flying pancake, raining food, bread boats, etc.). List these reasons on a chart entitled Tall Tale Exaggerations.

Read some other classic tall tales with your class. These can include stories about Paul Bunyan, John Henry, and Pecos Bill. Talk about these stories and why they are considered tall tales. Add these reasons to your chart.

| Character | Setting | Exaggeration |
|---|---|---|
| Marvelous Marty | Deep in a forest | |

Give the students an opportunity to write a tall tale. Help them organize their thoughts by folding their paper into three columns. Label the columns *character, setting,* and *exaggeration.* Direct them to fill in the columns by using information on the class Tall Tale Exaggerations chart or their own ideas. Then, using their information, have them write a story.

Some ideas for stories include:

- The Day the Rain Fell Up Instead of Down
- My Wild Pet, Tornado Tilly
- A Tornado Drank Up the Ocean
- The Day We Had No Weather

Children may draw a picture to illustrate their story.

# Adventure Story Starters

"...took the absolute necessities with them, and set sail on their rafts for a new land." This is how the people of Chewandswallow sailed away on a peanut butter sandwich boat and began a new adventure.

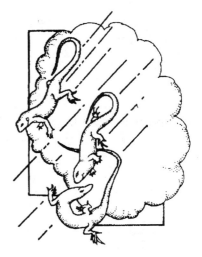

Have you ever imagined that you might have the kinds of weather adventures that the people in Chewandswallow had every breakfast, lunch, and dinner? Would you like to have this type of adventure?

Working in small groups choose one of the story starters below and write a story, letting your imaginations be the only thing to keep you grounded. Share finished stories with your class.

**Directions:** Cut out the story starters. Mount onto stiff paper. Assign one to each group to begin a story.

1. Once it rained fish in Louisiana! It really did. Once it rained lizards in Montreal, Canada! It really did. You are in Montreal when it begins to rain, and you look out your window and see it is raining live lizards. Oh my, . . .

2. Herbie is not the boy down the street. A Herbie is a wall of snow that suddenly smashes into you. You are outside playing on a sunny winter day. Suddenly you are hit by a Herbie and . . .

3. There is a terrible thunderstorm. Suddenly you look up and see lightning balls. They are red, yellow, and orange, and as large as grapefruits. They are glowing in the sky and seem to be heading your way . . .

4. Sometimes hailstones get trapped in a cloud. They are pushed up and down by strong air currents. Each time they go up, another layer of water freezes on them. The hailstones get so heavy, they fall to the ground. Sometimes they get sucked up so hard, they shoot out the top of the cloud. You're in a plane during a hailstorm. Your plane has trouble and you parachute out. You get trapped in a cloud. You feel . . .

5. A tornado is a very powerful, twisting wind storm. The winds around the center of a tornado go more than 300 miles per hour. Tornadoes uproot trees, destroy buildings, and carry cars. You have a tornado for a pet. You decide to take it for a walk in your neighborhood, and . . .

# After It Rains!

It is almost dinner time in the town of Chewandswallow. What would you like to see the skies rain down for dinner? Think about your ideal dinner and then draw it as it lands on the streets of Chewandswallow.

10

# Food Forecasting

Have students work by themselves, with a partner, or in a small group to forecast the "weather" in Chewandswallow. Predict the weather (menu) for one school day and one weekend day. Include breakfast, lunch, and dinner in the forecast. Write weather predictions for the two days below. When the students are finished, share the forecasts.

## Weather (Menu) Forecast

| School Day | Weekend Day |
|---|---|
| **Breakfast** | **Breakfast** |
| | |
| **Lunch** | **Lunch** |
| | |
| **Dinner** | **Dinner** |
| | |
| **Snack** | **Snack** |

# Physical Activities

## North, South, East, West Game

Discuss how you can tell directions. (The sun rises in the east and sets in the west. Facing east, south is to the right, north is to the left.)

Establish directions in the gym or play area. Identify the north, south, east, and west walls. The children must run and touch the correct wall as you call the directions. They must not touch each other. This is a non-competitive, warm-up game.

## Flying Pancakes

Play this game outside on a large field.

Divide the children into small groups. Give each group a flying disk or stiff paper plate. Ask each group to stand in a large circle. Toss the "flying pancake" around the circle. This is a non-competitive game.

## Pass the Hamburger

Play this game inside. Ask the children to find a partner. Give each pair an inflated balloon. Imagine the balloon is a hamburger. Have partners pass the hamburger back and forth. Don't let the "hamburger" land on the ground and get all dirty!

## Toss the Salad!

Divide the children into small groups. Give each group a medicine ball. (Check with your physical education teacher or department for a medicine ball.)

Imagine the ball is a giant tomato. Pass the tomato around the group. Don't let it land on your toes!

## Creative Movement

Challenge the children to move about the gym, imagining that they are various foods falling from the sky. Have them pretend to be a flying pancake, syrup, a tomato tornado, or a food of their choice.

# The Cloud Book

*by Tomie dePaola*

## Summary

*The whimsical illustrations combine with a humorous style to tell about clouds in a variety of ways. Best of all, Mr. dePaola provides wonderful metaphors for types of clouds, allowing young readers to imagine and remember their forms better. Children will delight in the "light touch" given to the presentation of the factual information and teachers will appreciate the ease with which their students can learn.*

The outline below is a suggested plan for using the various activities that are presented in this unit. You should adapt these ideas to fit your own classroom situation.

## Sample Plan

**Day 1**

- Read *The Cloud Book.*
- Discuss types of clouds.
- Study photographs of clouds.
- Complete Reading for Information. (page 18)
- Conduct the science experiment You Can Make Clouds. (page 42)
- Do Cloudy Words. (page 30)
- Go for a walk to observe clouds.
- Paint clouds. (page 51)
- Begin My Weather Dictionary. (page 29)

**Day 2**

- Review *The Cloud Book.*
- Discuss myths.
- Make up and record a class silly myth. (page 15)
- Begin Weather Myth Big Books. (page 24)
- Share them with the class.
- Read *The Hammer of Thunder* by Ann Pyk.
- Complete New Cloud Words. (page 31)
- Conduct experiment: You Can Make Rain. (page 42)
- Learn about The Water Cycle. (page 45)

**Day 3**

- Review *The Cloud Book.*
- Discuss funny sayings. Make some up in class.
- Complete Sayings About Weather. (page 19)
- Read *A January Fog Will Freeze a Hog and Other Weather Folklore* by Hubert Davis.
- Continue writing Weather Myth Big Books. (page 24)
- Discuss rainbows.
- Complete Rainbows and Wind. (page 28)
- Continue My Weather Dictionary. (page 29)

# Overview of Activities

## SETTING THE STAGE

1. Prepare your classroom for a unit on weather. Assemble bulletin board. Directions and patterns are given on pages 71–78.

2. Create a Library Corner. Collect photographs, fiction books, and non-fiction books about weather and display.

3. Display photographs of weather instruments, satellites, and weather stations. Set out basic weather instruments such as thermometers, barometers, rain gauges, etc. Have books offering weather experiments available.

4. Put out a large wall map and a set of small maps of North America (sample on page 48). Include a globe if possible. Supply a daily newspaper for the weather report.

5. Supply a radio and a schedule so the children can listen to the daily weather report.

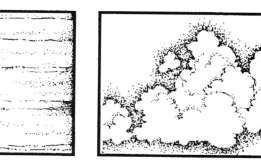

6. Collect and display photographs of cloud formations. (Ansel Adams photographs are a good source.) Set out labels naming the types of clouds. Ask the children to match labels to photographs. Later on, add a camera. Ask one or two children to photograph local clouds.

**cirrus**          **stratus**          **cumulus**

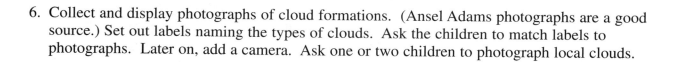

# Overview of Activities *(cont.)*

## ENExxNG THE BOOK

**ENJOYING THE BOOK**

1. Read the entire book to the class. Reread the first part of the book to the class. This part offers factual information about clouds. Discuss the various types of clouds, asking questions to encourage recall of information. Do the activity pages, Reading For Information (page 18) and What's That Cloud? (page 67).

2. Reread the second part of the book to the class. This section offers myths about weather. Discuss what makes myths and legends. Read one or two other myths (see Bibliography). Make up a few silly myths cooperatively. Record these on the blackboard. Do the activity page Weather Myth Big Books (page 24).

3. Students can decorate a large, folded piece of construction paper as a cover for a folder in which to collect their papers. These can be stapled together to form a Weather Booklet to keep all activity pages together.

4. Reread the third part of the book to the class. This part offers sayings about weather. Discuss how such sayings come about. Debate whether these sayings are true or not. Make up a few silly sayings cooperatively. Record them on the blackboard. Do the activity page, Sayings About Weather (page 19).

5. Reread the fourth part of the book to the class. This part offers a silly cloud story. Evaluate the story. Discuss different ways it could have been written. As a class, write your own silly cloud story.

# Overview of Activities *(cont.)*

---

## EXTENDING THE BOOK

1. Have a group discussion. Let the children answer the question "What Is Weather?" Help them develop a definition. Record it on a chart and display.

> ### What Is Weather?
>
> Weather is when it
> is rainy and . . .

2. As a language arts activity, let the class play with weather words. Have them complete Cloudy Words (page 30) and Weather Word Match (page 27).

3. Complete My Weather Dictionary found on page 29.

4. Tell the story of Jack Frost to the class. Let them talk about him. Have them write a Jack Frost story (page 25).

5. Write out labels for different types of clouds. Study cloud photographs and match them to the labels. Photograph unusual cloud formations and share them with the class.

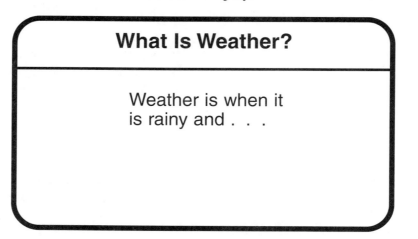

6. Do the experiments You Can Make Clouds and You Can Make Rain on page 42. Conduct several of the science experiments on pages 33–44.

7. Keep track of the daily temperature using the graph on page 32.

8. Make a breezy mobile (page 55), wind chimes (page 53), and a kite (page 53).

9. Choose some snowmen activities (page 52) to complete.

10. Paint with rain. Paint a picture with poster paints on white paper. After it dries, take it out in the rain. Holding it flat, let it catch some raindrops. See what happens.

11. Write and sing weather songs.

12. Have students Weather the Obstacles. (pages 62)

13. Do some creative movement (page 61). Choose different types of weather and move like them.

14. Culminating Activity—Become Weather Wizards (page 63). Learn to observe, record, and predict the weather.

# Myths About Weather

Long ago when people didn't understand something, they made up an imaginary tale to explain it. In *The Cloud Book,* the author talks about weather myths.

Write a myth of your own.

1. Read *The Hammer of Thunder* retold by Ann Pyk. (See bibliography.)

2. Reread the myth in *The Cloud Book.*

3. Imagine you lived long before there were meteorologists to help explain the weather. Now imagine that suddenly there was a terrible tornado. After it was over, all your friends and family tried to figure out what had happened and why. Put your ideas into a web. Now use your ideas to write a story.

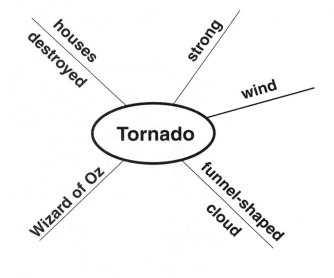

Use the blank web to collect your ideas to write a story. Make your story into a book by adding a cover. Share it with friends.

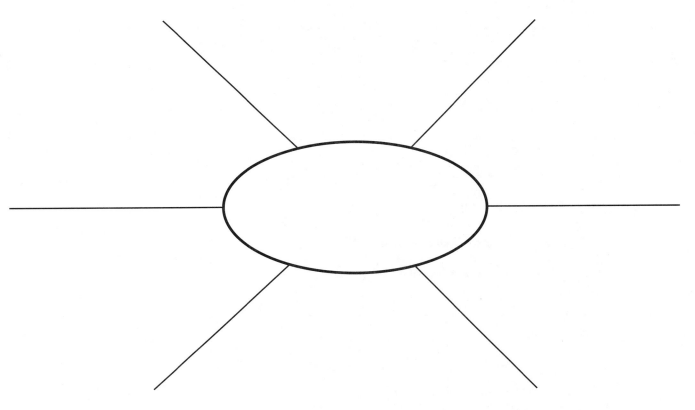

Some topics for weather myths include: lightning, hail, rainbows, hurricanes, and snow.

# Reading for Information

*The Cloud Book* by Tomie dePaola is a nonfiction book. It gives you a lot of information about clouds.

Read the book to find the answers to these questions.

1. What are clouds? _____

2. List the three main kinds of clouds _____

_____ , and _____ .

Label the pictures of the clouds.

a. _____  b. _____  c. _____

3. The highest clouds, sometimes known as "mare's tails" are called

_____ .

4. Fluffy clouds that look like cauliflower are called _____

_____ .

5. Clouds that look like gray blankets are called _____

_____ .

6. What is fog? _____

_____

_____

_____

# Sayings About Weather

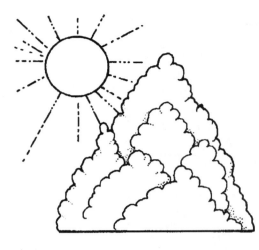

There are many humorous sayings about the weather such as:

"Red In the morning, sailors take warning, red at night, sailor's delight," or "It's raining cats and dogs."

The saying "In the morning, mountains, in the evening, fountains" appears in *The Cloud Book.*

Read *The Cloud Book* out loud and discuss it.  Then answer the questions.

1. What kind of clouds are like "mountains"? _____

   _____

2. What kind of weather do "mountains"of clouds bring?_____

   _____

3. What do you think the saying means? _____

   _____

4. Do you think this saying does a good job in forecasting the weather? _____

   Why? _____

5. Find the rhyming words from the sayings given in the book.  Write the rhyming word underneath the word.

   | hoppin' | mountains | gray | red | tails |
   |---|---|---|---|---|
   | _____ | _____ | _____ | _____ | _____ |

6. Write some funny sayings of your own about the weather on the back of this paper.

# Weather Poems

Read these weather poems with your class.

It's raining, it's pouring,

The old man is snoring.

He got into bed

And bumped his head

And couldn't get up in the morning.

One misty, moisty morning,

When cloudy was the weather,

I met a little old man

Clothed all in leather.

He began to compliment,

And I began to grin,

How do you do, and how do you do,

And how do you do again?

—*Tomie dePaola's Mother Goose.* Putnam, 1985. (Other versions of Mother Goose rhymes may be used.)

Read the poems with your class. Ask the class some questions: What weather words are used? Who is the old man in each poem? What type of weather is described in each poem?

With the class, make a Venn diagram comparing and contrasting the two poems.

## Shape Poem

A shape poem is written as a picture of the subject it's about. It is easier to write the words first and then form them into a shape. For example:

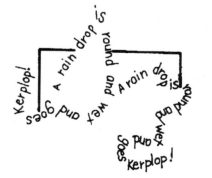

A rain drop is round and wet and goes kerplop!

Choose some weather words such as puddle, snowflake, rainbow, and sun, and write some shape poems.

# Write a Rain Poem

Read poems and stories about rain.  Brainstorm and collect colorful rain words.  Print them on a list called "rainy words." Have students use this list to help write a rain poem.  Children may print their poems in the umbrella.

# Weather Walks

Take an outing with your students by going on a weather walk. Let them experience the various types of weather. Make sure that they are dressed appropriately for the weather.

## Wind Walk

**Preparation:** Read *Gilberto and the Wind* by Marie Hall Ets. Make a chart listing windy words. Use these for spelling and creative writing. Include descriptive and sound words.

- Go for a Wind Walk! Stand very still and close your eyes. What do you feel? Let the wind touch your face. Watch the trees dance and listen to the leaves sing. What do you hear?

- Find a leaf. Toss it up into the wind. Watch where it goes.

- Stop. Watch the clouds race about. Where are they going?

- Watch the clouds transform into imaginary creatures.

- Put your back to the wind and let it push you about. Put the wind to your face and try to run forward into the wind.

- Find a maple leaf "helicopter" seed. Toss it high in the air. Try to catch it. Try this with pussy willows or milkweed.

- Make a paper airplane and toss it into the wind. What happens?

- Make a kite and run like the wind!

## Snow Walk

**Preparation:** Read *The Snowy Day* by Ezra Jack Keats.

- Go for a Snow Walk! Be a snow detective! Find prints or marks in the snow. What made the prints?

- Play geometric tag! The teacher leads the children, tramping out a large triangle, a square, and a circle shape. Divide into 3 groups. Assign each group to play on a shape. Choose someone in each group to be "It." The children must stay on the tracks.

- Have a snow picnic outside on shower curtains.

- Take sand shovels and pails outside and build snow castles.

# Weather Walks *(cont.)*

## Rain Walk

**Preparation:** Read *James and the Rain* by Karla Kuskin. Make a chart listing as many rainy words as possible. Include descriptive and sound words. Use for creative writing and spelling activities.

- Go for a Rain Walk! Stand very still and close your eyes. What do you feel? What do you hear?

- Find a big puddle. What happens when raindrops hit the puddle? Run and splash through it! Stomp in it!

- What happens when raindrops land on your eyelashes? Can you catch a raindrop on your tongue? Watch the raindrops fall. Do they come straight down? Do they bounce? Can you make a raindrop change directions as it falls? Put up your umbrella. Close your eyes and listen. What do you hear? Can you hear a rhythm? What words describe the sounds?

- Build a dam using sticks, dirt, and stones. Watch where the water goes now. Make a hole in your dam. What happens?

- Find a place where the water is moving, making a baby river. Make a boat out of a stick or leaf. See if it floats. Have boat races.

- Get an old shower curtain or part of a plastic drop sheet. Take it outside in the rain. Lay it on the ground, leaving it with some folds and wrinkles. Guess where rivers and lakes will form. Were you right?

## Sun Walk

**Preparation:** Read *Summer* by P.D. Eastman. Make a chart listing as many sunny words as possible. Include descriptive words. Use for spelling and creative writing activities.

- Go for a Sun Walk! Stand outside, facing the sun. (**Note:** Do not have children look directly at the sun.) Close your eyes. What do you feel?

- Lie on the grass and watch the clouds. What do they look like? Imagine they are something else.

- Go to the beach. Build sandcastles. Draw in the sand. Watch the sunshine sparkle on the waves.

- Play with shadows. Find the tiniest, biggest, fattest, and thinnest shadows you can. Make your own shadow big, small, fat, skinny, short, and tall. Make your shadow go in front of you and then behind you. How did you do it? Can you make your shadow disappear? Make funny shadows.

# Weather Myth Big Books

Children will enjoy creating Weather Myth Big Books to share with each other and other classes.

**Materials:** chart paper; markers, colored pencils, or crayons

Divide the children into three groups. With the class, brainstorm ideas for a weather myth. From the list, let the children choose an idea for their Big Book. Write a group composition, recording the rough copy on the board or chart paper. Edit and improve the story together. Decide together where to divide it into pages. Assign one group to copy the story onto large chart pages. Assign another group to illustrate each page. Assign a third group to "publish" cooperatively their story as a Big Book by making a title page that includes title, authors, illustrators, publishers, and date of publication. They may wish to have a page at the end called "Authors and Illustrators" that each student signs. Bind the book by punching two or three holes and using heavy yarn or rings to put it together.

## What If?

Ask the children to turn on their imaginations and write fiction stories. Suggest some of the following ideas:

What if snow fell in huge snowballs?

What if rain fell up instead of down?

What if you could sit in a cloud?

# Jack Frost

Jack Frost is an imaginary character who decorates the world with frost and ice.  His father was a wind god named Kari and his son is called Snjo—snow in English.  No one has ever seen him because he is imaginary.

Imagine you met Jack Frost.  Write a story to tell what happened.  Illustrate your story.  Use the frame on this page.

# Amazing Weather Facts

Make a special spot on the blackboard or chart called "AMAZING!"

Print or post a new amazing fact in this spot each day. Read and discuss this amazing weather fact each day with your class.

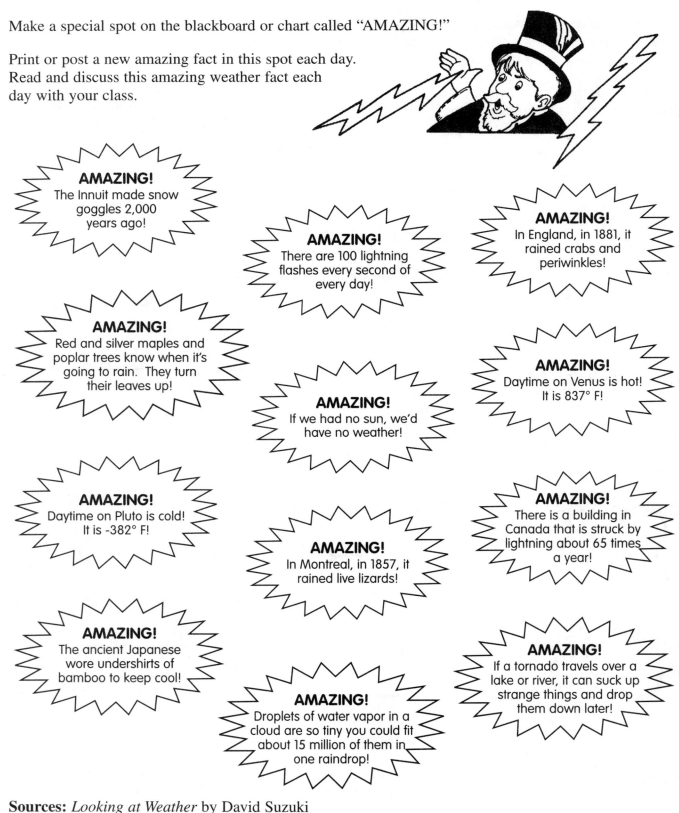

**AMAZING!**
The Innuit made snow goggles 2,000 years ago!

**AMAZING!**
There are 100 lightning flashes every second of every day!

**AMAZING!**
In England, in 1881, it rained crabs and periwinkles!

**AMAZING!**
Red and silver maples and poplar trees know when it's going to rain. They turn their leaves up!

**AMAZING!**
If we had no sun, we'd have no weather!

**AMAZING!**
Daytime on Venus is hot! It is 837° F!

**AMAZING!**
Daytime on Pluto is cold! It is -382° F!

**AMAZING!**
In Montreal, in 1857, it rained live lizards!

**AMAZING!**
There is a building in Canada that is struck by lightning about 65 times a year!

**AMAZING!**
The ancient Japanese wore undershirts of bamboo to keep cool!

**AMAZING!**
Droplets of water vapor in a cloud are so tiny you could fit about 15 million of them in one raindrop!

**AMAZING!**
If a tornado travels over a lake or river, it can suck up strange things and drop them down later!

**Sources:** *Looking at Weather* by David Suzuki

*Weather Watch* by Valerie Wyatt

26

# Weather Word Match

Draw lines to match the words and the definitions to the pictures.

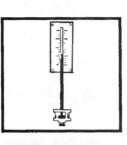

**barometer**

water that falls from clouds—
rain, snow, sleet, hail

**hurricane**

a person who studies weather

**meteorologist**

instrument for measuring
temperature

**thermometer**

violent thunderstorm with high
winds

**tornado**

instrument for measuring air
pressure

**precipitation**

very violent windstorm

# Rainbows and Wind

Discuss what causes a rainbow. (It is caused when sunlight shines on raindrops.) Ask the children to define a rainbow. Record their ideas and help them develop a cooperative definition. Print this on a rainbow shaped chart.

Read the story *A Rainbow of My Own* by Don Freeman. After reading it, ask the children to turn on their imaginations. Ask "What if you had a rainbow of your very own?" Brainstorm, accepting all ideas. Have the children write stories about their ideas. Let them illustrate stories using markers or by painting rainbows using wet brush techniques. Share the stories with the class.

Do the same activity with the wind, explaining that wind is caused by cooler air pushing in to take the place of the warm air. Write the cooperative definition on a wind-shaped card (see p. 74). Read the story *The Wind and Me* by Beverly Butler. Ask them to answer "What does the wind look like?" to spark their imaginations.

## Bulletin Board Displays

### Rainbows

**Materials:** blue paper; crepe paper in assorted rainbow colors; tape or stapler

Cover the board with blue paper. Staple the class rainbow definition in one corner. Cut thin strips of crepe paper in rainbow colors. Around the board, tape or staple one piece of crepe paper at a time, twisting each gently. Staple up the stories and illustrations.

### Wind

**Materials:** blue paper; white crepe paper; tape or stapler

Cover the bulletin board with blue paper. Staple the class chart defining wind in one corner. Cut strips of white crepe paper. Staple one end of each strip to the wind shaped card. Pull each strip out in a fan shape, twisting gently, and staple the end. Staple up the stories and illustrations.

# My Weather Dictionary

Make a dictionary of weather definitions.  Start with these and add some of your own,

**Directions:** Cut out each definition.  Paste each one onto pages in a mini booklet made by folding a sheet of paper in half horizontally, then vertically.  Staple as many as needed.  Draw a picture for each definition.  Add some words and definitions of your own.  Title the booklet "My Weather Dictionary."

## What is Wind?

Warm air rises.  Cool air moves down. They mix and push together.  If they move fast, it is called wind.

## What is Rain?

Air holds moisture.  If the air cools, or if it is holding too much moisture, the air drops the moisture.  This can make rain.

## What is Lightning?

Lightning is a giant spark of electricity flashing through the sky.  It heats the air so much and so quickly that we can see the hot air.

## What is Thunder?

The giant spark of electricity makes the air so hot so quickly, that the air bumps into the cooler air around it. And it bumps so hard, that it makes a cracking sound. This is called thunder.

## What is a Rainbow?

If there are many droplets of rain in the air, and the sun comes out, then the sunlight shines through the droplets of rain. The water droplet acts like a prism, splitting the white light into all its colorful parts.

## What is Snow?

Sometimes the water in the air is frozen into tiny ice crystals. When these fall, they are called snow.

# Cloudy Words

How many words can you make using the letters from the cloud word *cumulonimbus*?

Print one word in each cloud.

# New Cloud Words

A. **Directions:** Make new words by joining one word part from column 1 with one word part from column 2.

| Column 1 | Column 2 | |
| --- | --- | --- |
| Alto | cumulus | _____ |
| Cirro | stratus | _____ |
| Cumulo | nimbus | _____ |
| Strato | cumulus | _____ |

B. **Directions:** Using *The Cloud Book* or any other books on clouds, list the names of other clouds.

_____   _____

_____   _____

_____   _____

_____   _____

# What Is the Temperature?

You will need several weather thermometers for this activity.

## Directions

1. Find a safe place outside to put your thermometer.
2. Note the temperature at the same time each day.
3. Put a dot on the graph to show the temperature for the day.
4. Connect the dots for a line graph.

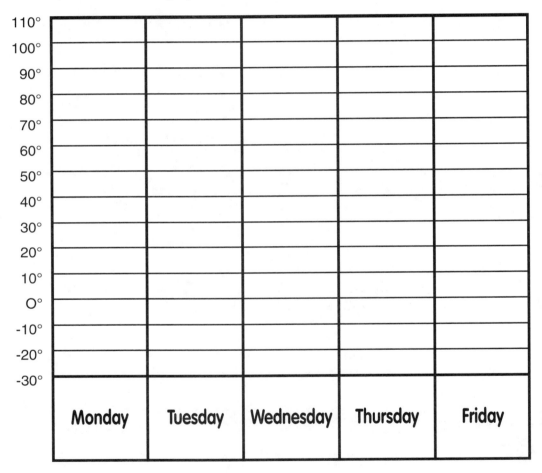

## Extensions

Compare temperatures in the morning, at lunchtime, and in the afternoon.

Compare your findings with local weather forecasts.

Put several thermometers in various settings. Compare readings.

Use subtraction skills to find how much hotter/cooler temperatures are when making the comparisons above. Make bar graphs to show the comparisons.

# Make a Rain Gauge

## Materials

funnel; masking tape; permanent marking pen; ruler; tall narrow jar with straight sides (an olive jar works well)

## Preparation

1. Ask the children or parents to collect suitable jars.

2. Find a flat, open area outside, clear of trees, roofs, and bushes. Ensure it is a safe place where the rain gauges won't be disturbed.

*Believe it or not!*
Once in Maryland, it rained 1.22 inches in one minute!

## Directions

1. Cut a strip of masking tape as long as your jar. Lay it on your table or desk.

2. Mark it off in ½" sections using your ruler and a pen. Stick this onto the outside of your jar.

3. Print your name in ink onto another piece of masking tape. Stick this onto the jar.

4. Place the funnel into the top of the jar. Tape it in place if necessary.

5. Carry your rain gauge carefully outside to the safe open place.

6. Check it each day at the same time to see how much rain has fallen.

7. Record your findings onto the rain graph. (page 34)

8. Empty your rain gauge to start again.

9. Use subtraction to compare your findings with a weather report.

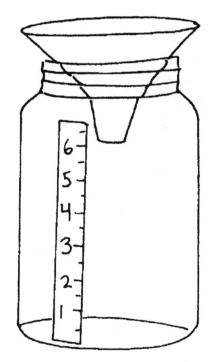

*Believe it or not!*
Once in Africa, it did not rain at all for 14 years!

# Rain Bar Graph

| Inches of Rain | Monday | Tuesday | Wednesday | Thursday | Friday | | Monday | Tuesday | Wednesday | Thursday | Friday |
|---|---|---|---|---|---|---|---|---|---|---|---|
| 5 | | | | | | | | | | | |
| 4½ | | | | | | | | | | | |
| 4 | | | | | | | | | | | |
| 3½ | | | | | | | | | | | |
| 3 | | | | | | | | | | | |
| 2½ | | | | | | | | | | | |
| 2 | | | | | | | | | | | |
| 1½ | | | | | | | | | | | |
| 1 | | | | | | | | | | | |
| ½ | | | | | | | | | | | |
| 0 | | | | | | | | | | | |

**Extension:** Listen to the weather report on the radio or television or read it in the newspaper for two weeks. Record the amount of rain or snow, and then graph it. **Note:** You may wish to enlarge the graph and do this as a class activity.

34

# Measure Snow

## Materials

clear 8 oz. measuring cups; balances or utility scales

## Directions

1. Go outside and measure 1 cup of snow. Bring it inside.

2. How much does it weigh?

   It weighs _____.

3. Set it on a table to melt.

4. How much water is in the cup?

   One cup of snow equals _____ cups of water.

5. Weigh the cup of water (melted snow).

   It weighs _____.

6. Did the weight change when it melted?

## Challenge

Try to find out if a loose cupful of snow weighs the same as a tightly packed cupful of snow. Note: If you don't have any snow, try crushed ice.

**Believe it or not!**
One winter on Mt. Rainier, 83 feet of snow fell. That's enough to cover a four story building.

# Which Way the Wind?

A wind vane is an instrument that tells which direction—north, south, east, west—the wind is blowing.

## Materials

large darning needles; 6" (15 cm) squares of cardboard; plastic drinking straws; empty spools of thread; markers; scissors; paste or tape; clay

## Preparation

Find a safe place outside for the children to keep their wind vanes. Trace the arrow below onto stiff paper for the children to use as a template. Divide the children into groups of 3 or 4 and give each a set of materials.

## Directions

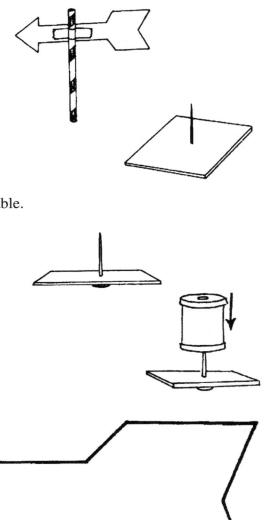

1. Make an arrow, using the pattern. Color and cut it out.

2. Paste or tape the arrow to one end of the straw.

3. Carefully push the darning needle through the piece of cardboard, so that it sticks straight up and is almost all the way through.

4. Push a small piece of clay onto the bottom of the needle.

5. Flatten the clay by pushing the cardboard down on the table. The cardboard should sit flat on the table. Print your names on the cardboard.

6. Put a spool over the needle.

7. Slip the straw over the needle. Make sure the straw can turn easily. Now take your wind vane outside. Find a place to put it where the wind can blow. It should be out in the open, where it will not be disturbed. What happens when the wind blows? How can you tell which direction the wind is blowing?

# How Hard Does the Wind Blow?

An anemometer is a wind gauge that tells how hard the wind is blowing.

## Materials

4 paper cups; 12" (30 cm) square of cardboard; 18" (46 cm) dowel; long straight pin; pencil; bead; ruler

## Preparation

Divide the class into small groups of 3 or 4, giving each a set of materials.

## Directions

1.  Using a ruler, draw a diagonal line across the cardboard, corner to corner.

2.  Draw another diagonal line across, joining the other two corners.

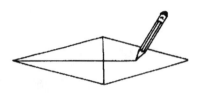

3.  Tape or glue a cup on each corner of the cardboard square.

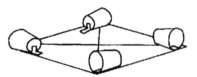

4.  Poke the pin down through the center of the cardboard, where the lines cross.

5.  Put the pin through the bead.

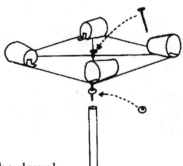

6.  Gently tap the pin into the tip of the dowel.

7.  Now take your wind gauge outside and look for some wind.

# Where Does the Wind Blow?

A wind sock shows the direction of the wind. It also shows the strength of the wind.

## Materials

old shirt sleeve; 16" (40 cm) of firm, lightweight wire; cotton thread; scissors; sewing needle; small stone

## Preparation

Ask parents to contribute old, long-sleeved shirts. Divide the children into groups of 3 or 4. Give each group a set of materials. Find two trees in an open area. Tie a rope between the two.

## Directions

1. Cut the shirt sleeves in half vertically.

2. Bend the wire into a circle.

3. Pull one open end of the sleeve over the wire circle.

4. Place stone into the hem near the wire circle. Sew or staple the overlapping edges to hold the stone and wire in place.

5. Stitch the other end of the sleeve closed.

6. Tie one end of the string to the circle, opposite the stone.

7. Tie your wind sock onto the rope outside.

   What does the wind sock tell you about the wind?

# Create the Wind

| Hot Air Spirals |
| --- |

Using the pattern below, create two different types of hot air spirals.

## Spiral 1

### Materials
markers; scissors; thread; paper; pattern

### Directions
1. Trace, color, and cut out the pattern below.
2. Poke a hole in the center of the spiral, between the XX.
3. Cut a piece of thread about 8" (20 cm) long.
4. Poke the thread through the hole and knot it.

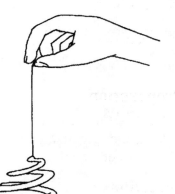

Hold the spiral by the thread.  Stand still.  What happens?

## Spiral 2

### Materials
lamp; pencil; scissors, paper; pattern

### Directions
1. Turn on the lamp.
2. Trace the pattern below.
3. Make a small bump on the XX.
4. Hold a pencil just above the light bulb.  (Don't burn yourself.)
5. Balance the XX mark of the spiral on the end of the pencil.

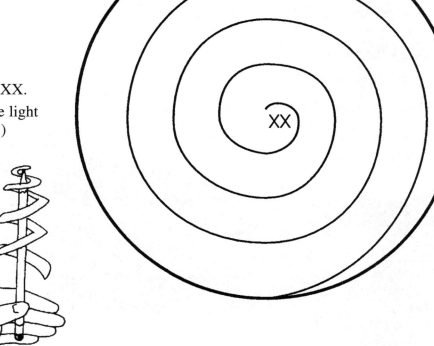

Hold the spiral above a heat register.  If hot air is blowing, how is the spiral's movement different than if there is only heat?

# High or Low?

A barometer measures how much the air is pushing down. In wet weather, the air pushes down a little. This is called low pressure. In dry weather, the air presses down a lot. This is called high pressure. A barometer can help you forecast the weather.

## Materials

round balloon; straw; jar with wide mouth; tape; strong elastic band; paper and pen

## Directions

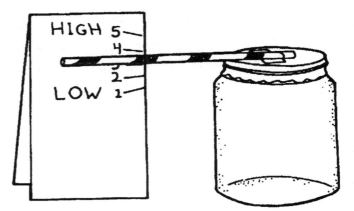

1. Working with a partner, have one partner stretch the balloon by blowing it up several times.

2. Cut off the neck of the balloon by cutting the balloon in half. Throw the neck away.

3. Ask your partner to help you stretch the balloon over the mouth of the jar.

4. Fasten it with the elastic band.

5. Tape the straw onto the balloon "lid" as shown.

6. Cut out a square of paper a little taller than your jar.

7. Mark the paper as shown.

8. Tape the paper to the wall.

9. Place your jar beside the paper.

Check your barometer each morning, using the chart on page 41 to record information. Did the straw move? Why?

**Believe it or not!**

There is over one ton of air on top of you right now!

# High or Low? *(cont.)*

Record the barometric pressure.

1. Check you barometer every day at the same time.
2. Record your findings below.
3. What kind of weather makes the straw point the highest?
4. What kind of weather makes the straw point the lowest?

| Day | Up (↑) or Down (↓) | Weather |
|-----|--------------------|---------|
|     |                    |         |
|     |                    |         |
|     |                    |         |
|     |                    |         |
|     |                    |         |
|     |                    |         |
|     |                    |         |

# Creating Weather

## You Can Make Clouds

A cloud is a huge crowd of tiny water droplets.

**Materials:** clean, self-sealing plastic bags; a freezer; air

**Directions:** Open a plastic bag and scoop some air into it.  Seal the bag tightly shut.  Put it in the freezer for 5 minutes.  After 5 minutes, take it out, open it, and blow into it.  Quickly seal it shut.

What happens? Why? How did you make a cloud?

## You Can Make Rain

Rain is drops of water falling from clouds.

**Materials:** jars with covers or lids; big bowls of ice

**Preparation:** Put out 3 or 4 bowls of ice.  Divide the children into groups of 3 or 4.  Give each group a jar with a lid.

**Directions:** Dry the outside of the jar.  Fill it with ice.  Put the lid on tightly.  What happens? Why? Draw what happened.

## You Can Make a Rainbow

A rainbow is caused by sunlight shining on raindrops.

**Materials:** bright sunshine; pocket mirrors; pans; jugs (to carry water); towel; pieces of white paper

**Preparation:** Divide children into small groups, giving each a set of materials.

**Directions:**

1. Place the pan where the sun can shine on it.

2. Fill the pan with water.

3. Place the mirror in the pan, under the water. Lean it against the side of the pan, at an angle.

4. Move the pan gently so the sun is shining directly on the mirror.

5. Move the mirror slightly until it reflects the light.  What happens? Why?

6. Try to catch the reflections of the colors on the white paper.

# Creating Weather *(cont.)*

## You Can Make Lightning

Lightning is caused by electricity.

**Materials:** wool or nylon carpet

**Directions:**

**Note:** Choose a cold, dry day to do this experiment.

1. Choose a partner.
2. Make the room as dark as possible.
3. Rub your feet back and forth on the carpet.
4. Touch your partner with one finger.

What did you feel? What did you see? Trade places. Now both of you rub your feet at the same time. Touch fingers. Tell what happened.

**Homework:** Make lightning in your mouth. To do this, you will need wintergreen Life Saver® candies and a mirror. Do this on a cold, dry day. Make the room as dark as possible. Chew on two wintergreen hard candies with your mouth wide open. Watch what happens in a mirror. Draw what you saw.

## You Can Make Frost

Frost is a covering of tiny ice crystals.

**Materials:** clean dry glass; 3 ice cubes; 3 tablespoons salt

**Preparation:** Divide the class into groups of 3 or 4. Give each group a set of materials.

**Directions:**

1. Make sure the glass is clean and dry.
2. Put 3 ice cubes in the glass.
3. Add 3 tablespoons of salt.
4. Observe what happens.
5. Wait a few minutes. Observe what happens now.
6. What did you make?

# Pollution Test

How much pollution is in the snow around you?

**Materials**

coffee filters; plastic cups; masking tape; pens; snow or rain

**Directions**

1. Scoop cupfuls of snow from various places in the schoolyard. Label each cup to show where you got it.

2. Take the samples into the classroom and let the snow melt.

3. Pour each sample through a separate coffee filter.

**Step 1**

**Answer the following questions:**

Which sample had the most pollution?

Which sample had the least pollution?

What do you think caused this pollution?

Discuss air pollution. What is it? What causes it? What does it do to us?

**Step 2**

Discuss local air pollution. Brainstorm with the children what they can do to decrease the area's air pollution.

Follow through on some ideas. It is important to show them that they can do something to improve their environment. This gives them a sense of citizen responsibility and a sense of hope.

Repeat this activity with rain samples.

Have students repeat this experiment as homework with snow or rain samples from around their homes. Have them bring in the results and share them with the class.

**Step 3**

# The Water Cycle

Where does the rain come from? Where does the rain go? Why do we never get any "new water"? Can you answer these questions? The water cycle answers them. Study the diagram below to learn how the water cycle works.

**Precipitation** is water that falls from the sky. It can be rain or snow. Color the precipitation dark gray.

**Water vapor** is water that has turned into gas. Clouds are made of water vapor. Color the clouds a light gray.

**Evaporation** is when water changes from liquid to gas. Color the evaporation light blue.

**Run-off** is the water that seeps into the ground, runs into rivers, or forms puddles. Color the run-off light brown.

# Where Will It Rain?

Look at the weather map on this page. Use the map to answer the questions.

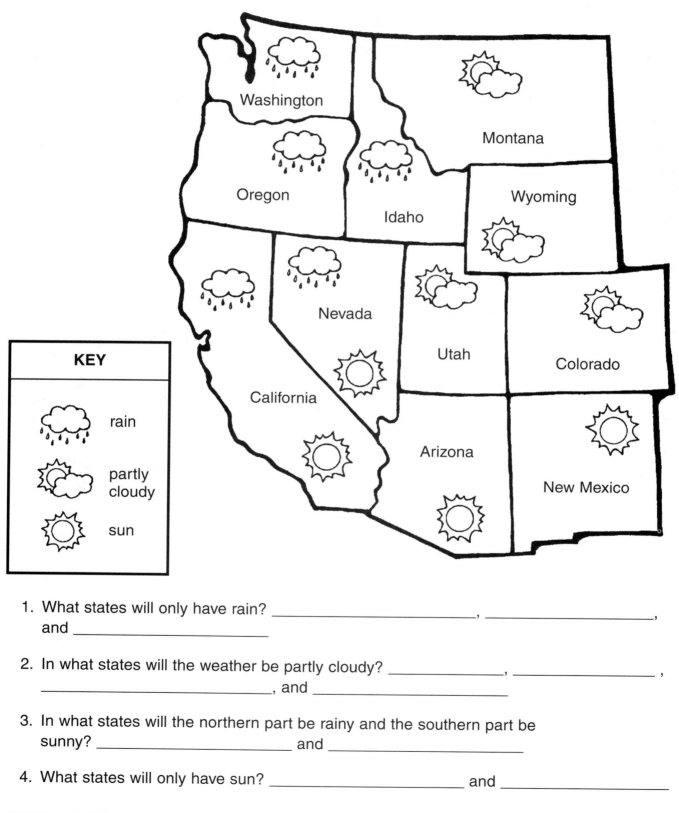

1. What states will only have rain? _____, _____, and _____

2. In what states will the weather be partly cloudy? _____, _____, _____, and _____

3. In what states will the northern part be rainy and the southern part be sunny? _____ and _____

4. What states will only have sun? _____ and _____

# The Weather Report

## Materials

Tape or pins; map of North America; weather symbols (see pages 48 and 49)

## Preparation

Discuss why weather is different in different places. How can we find out the weather in North America? What symbols could we use to report and record the weather on a map?

For homework, ask children to find out about the weather patterns in North America. Have them watch the TV weather report, listen to the radio, or read the newspaper report. Have them bring in the information about a specific date.

## Directions

Organize the children into small groups. Have each make a set of weather symbols. They may develop their own or use those given on page 49.

Color the symbols and mount on light cardboard. Cut them out. Laminate if possible.

---

### Create a Weather Report

---

Using information from their homework, ask children to report on the weather in North America on a chosen date. They should use the map from page 48 and their symbols.

Use blue yarn to show where a cold front is and yellow yarn to show where a warm front is. Add arrows to show which way the fronts are moving. They may add a large H to show High Pressure and a large L to show Low Pressure.

You may wish to do this as a small group activity for several days, with a different group reporting orally each day.

# The Weather Report *(cont.)*

## Map of North America

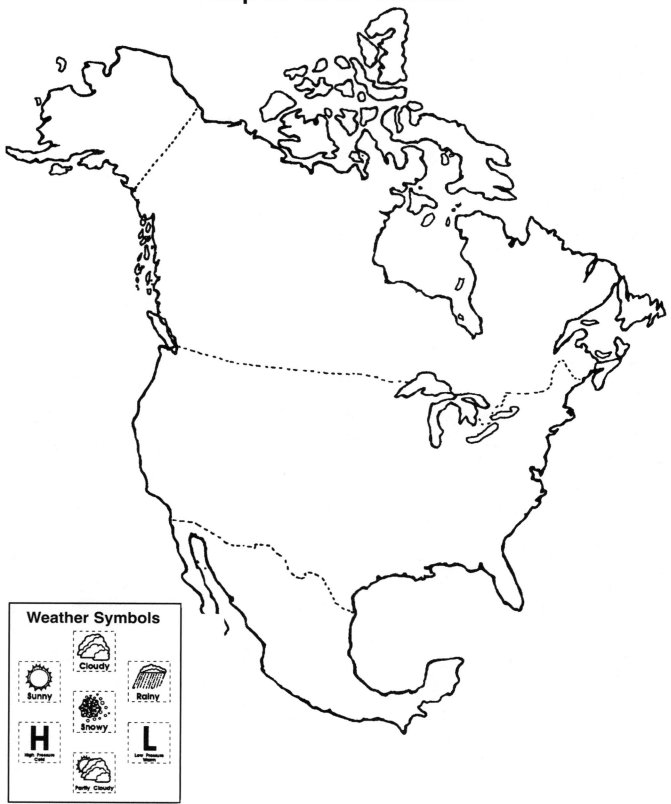

**Weather Symbols**

Sunny

Cloudy

Rainy

Snowy

H
High Pressure
Cold

L
Low Pressure
Warm

Partly Cloudy

# The Weather Report *(cont.)*

## Weather Symbols

Color and cut out.  Roll a small piece of masking tape and put on the back of each.  Stick these symbols onto the weather calendar (page 50) or reduce and use on the map of North America.

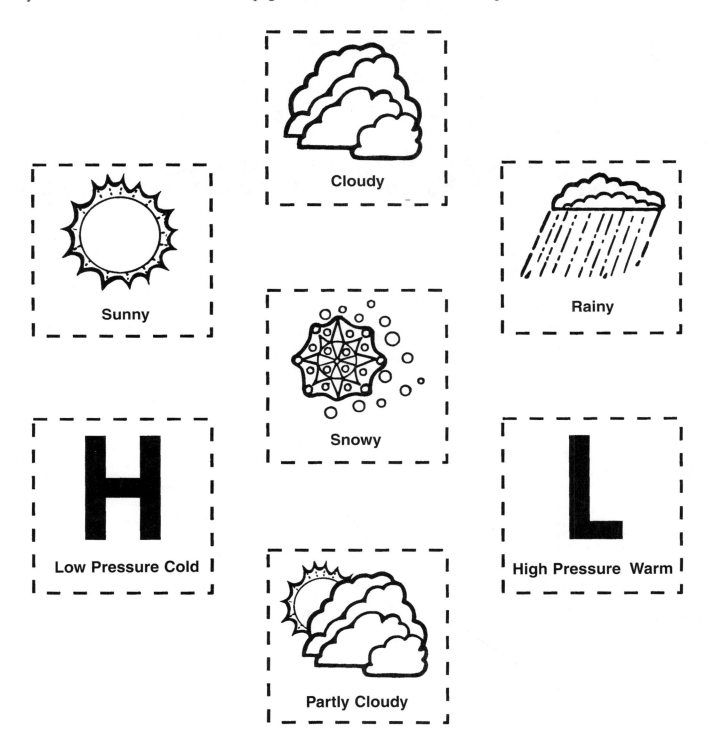

Cloudy

Sunny

Rainy

Snowy

**H** Low Pressure Cold

**L** High Pressure Warm

Partly Cloudy

# Weather Calendar

Use the calendar below to have students keep track of the daily weather. This can be done as an individual or class activity.

**Directions:** For individual charts, reproduce pages 49 and 50. You will need extra copies of page 49 if the weather is the same on consecutive days. Have children color, cut, and glue the appropriate symbol on each day of the week. They can complete a weather report form for each day.

To use as a class activity, enlarge the chart and symbols onto heavy paper. Color, cut out, and laminate. Attach Velcro® dots to the middle of each calendar box and to the middle of the back of the words and symbols. Hang the calendar in the classroom. Symbols and words can be placed in a box or envelope nearby. Attach the appropriate symbol each day. (**Note:** If out-of-the-ordinary weather conditions occur, you will have to create symbols for them.) The Weather Report can be reproduced onto chart paper and laminated for a wipe off form that can be changed each day.

| Monday | Tuesday | Wednesday | Thursday | Friday |
|--------|---------|-----------|----------|--------|
|        |         |           |          |        |

## Weather Report

Today is _____. It is _____ .
                      Day                                    Date

The weather is _____ .

# Painting Clouds!

## Materials

watercolors; paintbrushes; jars of water; 2 or 3 plastic drop sheets or old shower curtains; large sheets of white construction paper; pictures of storms, sunsets, sunrises.

## Preparation

1. Spread out the drop sheets and set out the materials.
2. Show the children pictures of storms, sunsets, sunrises.
3. Challenge them to be inventive—to get away from stereotypical blue sky and white clouds.
4. Divide them into 2 or 3 groups.

## Directions

**Wet Brush:** A Daytime Sky

1. Paint your paper with water first.
2. Paint clouds. Use lots of water.
3. Add some daytime colors on top.
4. Let your painting dry flat.

**Wet Brush:** A Sunrise or Sunset Sky

1. Paint your paper with water.
2. Paint clouds colored by a sunset, sunrise, or a storm.
3. Let your painting dry flat.

**Dry Brush:** On Top of Your Paintings

After your painting is dry, add finishing touches with a small paintbrush and a small paintbox of paints. This time use lots of paint and very little water! Your paintbrush will leave textured bristle marks. This technique is called Dry Brush.

Choose your best painting. Mount it on construction paper. Display it on the bulletin board.

Art

# Snowman Projects

## Unmeltable Snowman

### Materials

newspaper; safety pins; boots; 3 white pillowcases; scarf; construction paper; masking tape; hat; scissors

### Preparation

1. Divide the class into large groups.
2. Give each group a set of the materials and a large working space.

### Directions

1. Scrunch up single sheets of newspaper.
2. Stuff the three pillowcases with newspaper.
3. Tie the tops of the pillowcases shut.
4. Tape and pin the three "balls" together into a snowman shape.
5. Tie on the scarf and pin on the hat.
6. Make a face and buttons out of construction paper and tape on.
7. Make a sign to tell your snowman's name and who made him.

## Paper Bag Snowmen

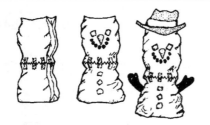

Build paper bag snowmen by stuffing white paper lunch bags with scrunched newspaper. Tape 2 bags together for each snowman. Decorate them with construction paper, yarn, cloth, sticks, etc.

## Marshmallow Snowmen

Give each child 2 stale marshmallows, toothpicks, scraps of yarn, ribbon, fabric, and felt pens. Stick a toothpick halfway into one marshmallow. Push the second marshmallow over the toothpick.

Draw a face and buttons onto the marshmallow with felt pens.

Glue or tie on scraps for a scarf and hat. Push tiny twigs or broken toothpicks into the marshmallow to make arms.

52

# Fun With Wind

## Let's Make a Kite!

### Materials

large plastic grocery bags; string; crepe or tissue paper; tape; wrapping paper scraps; tinfoil or cellophane

### Directions

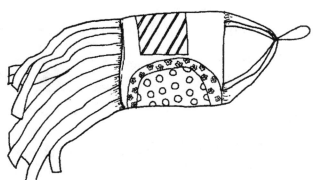

1. Fold the plastic bag flat.

   Tape on large paper scraps to decorate your bag.

2. Cut streamers out of crepe or tissue paper, tinfoil, or cellophane.

3. Tape the streamers to the bottom of the bag.

4. Cut a piece of string about 1 yard (1 meter) long.

5. Tie each end of the string onto the bag handle to form a large loop. Go outside and open the bag wide. Hold onto the string loop and go for a wind run!

## Make a Wind Chime

### Materials

large nails of various metals and sizes; string; scissors; cardboard 6" (15.24 cm) square

### Directions

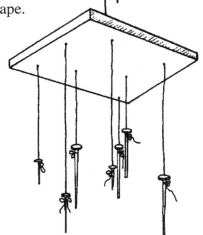

1. Poke several holes in the cardboard. Ensure that they are not too close together.

2. Thread a string though each hole in the cardboard and knot or tape.

3. Tie a nail to the end of each string.

4. Take your materials outside into the wind if you can.

5. Experiment with different kinds and sizes of nails.

6 Experiment with different lengths of string.

7. Hang your wind chime up outside, out of children's reach.

### Hot tip!

Make another wind chime using sea shells.

# Snowflake Activities

## Catch a Snowflake

**Materials:** black construction paper; magnifying glass

**Directions:**

1. Chill the construction paper by putting it in the freezer or leaving it outside in a sheltered, dry spot on a freezing day.

2. Catch falling snowflakes on the paper and examine them with the magnifying glass.

## Make Snowy Flakes

Snowflakes are crystals with six sides. No two are exactly alike.

**Materials:** pattern; scissors; colored tissue or construction paper; thread; tape

**Directions:**

Trace or duplicate the pattern below. Fold on the dotted lines. Cut out designs. Unfold and see what happens. (Note: For an easier snowflake, have students use a square, folded into fourths.)

Tape your favorite snowflakes to the windows, hang them from the ceiling, or tie them to a coat hanger and make a snowflake mobile.

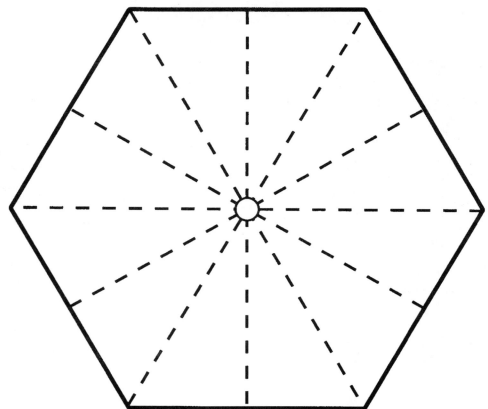

# Mobiles

## Breezy Mobile

### Materials

coat hanger; construction paper; scissors; thread; tape; small bells (optional)

### Directions

1. Color and cut out shapes. These can be circles, triangles, squares, or any other geometric shapes.
2. Carefully poke a hole into each shape.
3. Pull various lengths of thread through and knot or tape to the shape.
4. Tie the other end of the thread to the coat hanger.
5. Hang your mobile up where it can blow in the wind.
6. Tie small bells to your mobile if you like.

## Snowman Mobile

### Materials

stiff white paper; thread or yarn; colored construction paper; paste or glue

### Preparation

Reproduce the patterns (pages 56 and 57) onto stiff white paper. Tie a long string across the room high enough to hang up the mobiles.

### Directions

1. Cut out all the pattern pieces.
2. Draw eyes, nose, and mouth onto the smallest circle. Draw buttons on the other two circles.
3. Paste the scarf onto the head and the arms onto the middle-sized circle.
4. Using your pencil point, punch holes in the top and bottom of each mobile part.
5. Attach the circles together with thread or yarn, according to the diagram, so they hang free from each other.
6. Print your name on the back. Now hang up your snowman mobile!

# Snowman Mobile *(cont.)*

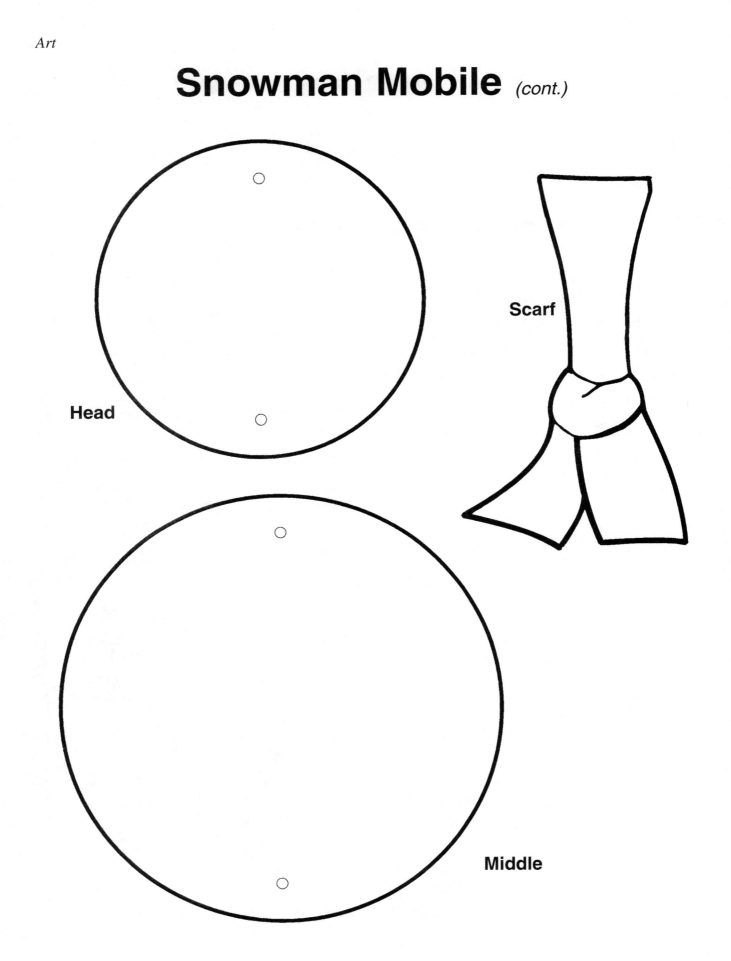

Head

Scarf

Middle

# Snowman Mobile *(cont.)*

**Hat**

**Arms**

**Bottom**

# Weather Songs

Sing the following songs with your class.

**Fun in the Rain!** *(Tune: "Three Blind Mice")*

Rain, rain, rain

Rain, rain, rain

Dribble, dribble sploosh!

Dribble, dribble sploosh!

Grab your boots, your coat, and hat,

Jump in a puddle and go kersplat!

Stomp about and become a drowned rat,

Rain, rain, rain.

Rain, rain, rain.

**Lacy Snowflakes** *(Tune: "London Bridge Is Falling Down")*

Lacy snowflakes falling down,

Falling down, falling down,

Lacy snowflakes falling down,

Tickly, tingly snowflakes.

Now try writing some weather songs of your own! Follow these steps and write a song about the snow.

1. Brainstorm with your class some ideas and words that tell about snow. Record these on the board or a chart.

2. Review the tune and rhythm of "Three Blind Mice."

3. Write these lines on the board for students to see.

    Here comes snow,

    Here comes snow.

    _____

    _____

    _____

    _____

    _____

    That was snow.

    That was snow.

> ### Sing Some Weather Songs!
>
> Sing some songs about the weather. *Everybody Sings,* compiled by Debbie Coyle (DMC Publications, Fort Collins, Colorado), has a section of weather songs. Don't forget to sing some classic favorites too, like "The Eency, Weency Spider," "You Are My Sunshine," "Frosty the Snowman," and "Raindrops Keep Falling on My Head."

4. Using some ideas from the brainstorming list, have the class fill in the blank lines in the rhythm of the song.

5. Sing the song the class has written.

Try this activity to the tune of "London Bridge," "Mary Had a Little Lamb," or any other familiar rhyme.

# Let's Cook With Snow

Divide the children into groups of 4 or 5. Give each group a plastic bag containing a set of the materials. Take them outside. Turn a snowy place into a kitchen.

**Note:** You will need fresh, clean snow. If you doubt that the available snow is fresh and clean, or you have no snow available, make your own. To do this, give each group a bag of ice and a rubber mallet or hammer. Ask the children to wrap the bag of ice in a towel. Have them take turns hitting the ice with the hammer.

Or, simply buy bags of crushed ice to use in place of snow.

## Snow Sherbet

### Materials

clean, fresh snow; reusable plastic cups; measuring spoons; powdered juice mix

### Directions

1. Spoon 2 tablespoons of clean snow into a cup.

2. Stir in 1 teaspoon juice powder.

3. Enjoy!

## Snow Cream

### Materials

clean, fresh snow; cream; large plastic mixing bowl; plastic measuring cups; large spoon; maple syrup; spoons; plastic cups for dishes

### Directions

1. Put 1 cup of clean snow in a bowl.

2. Pour ¼ cup cream over the snow.

3. Add ⅓ cup maple syrup a little at a time, stirring slowly.

4. Serve a little snow cream to each person.

# Wind Game

## Materials

paper; tape; chairs; string about 6 feet/1.82 m

## Directions

Divide the class into two teams.

Each team must do the following.

1. Cut out one 5" (12.70 cm) square of paper.

2. Shape the square into a cone and tape it.

3. Tie a long piece of string onto one chair.

   Pass the string through the cone and tie onto a second chair.

4. Position the chairs about 6 feet/1.82 m apart.

5. Position the cone near one chair, with the tip pointing to the other chair.

6. Take turns blowing to make the cone move to the other end.

7. Have a Wind Relay Race against the other team! Ask one person to say "Ready, set, go!" Each person on your team must blow the cone to the other end and then push it back to the beginning with his hand.

8. Have a Cooperative Wind Race against the other team! Figure out a way that your team can work cooperatively to blow the cone to the other end. Perhaps it will be a few people at a time, or all together. Explain your cooperative plan to the other team. See which team can blow the cone to the end first.

# Weather Games

## Lightning Relay

Divide the class into two teams. Each team stands in a line and holds hands. Send the "lightning shock"—a gentle hand squeeze—down the line. When the last person receives the squeeze, he or she runs to the head of the line. He or she then sends the lightning shock down again. When everyone is back in his or her original position, the team sits down.

## Creative Weather Movement

Try some creative movement with the children. Give them paper streamers, one for each hand. Set the movement to music. Classical music often works well for this. Try some of the following:

Be a snowflake fluttering slowly down, twirling around.

Be a bolt of lightning shooting down.

Be a hailstone smashing down.

Be the wind blowing all about.

## Netting Notions

Use netting to help students see how the wind blows. Give each student a foot square piece of veil netting. Let them throw it in the air. Ask them "How does it come down?" Throw it in the air again. Turn around. "Did the wind blow it down before you could catch it?"

# Weather the Obstacles

Set up an obstacle course in the gym as shown. Spread the children around the course. They may start anywhere, but need to rotate in order. Let them have fun challenging themselves to do well.

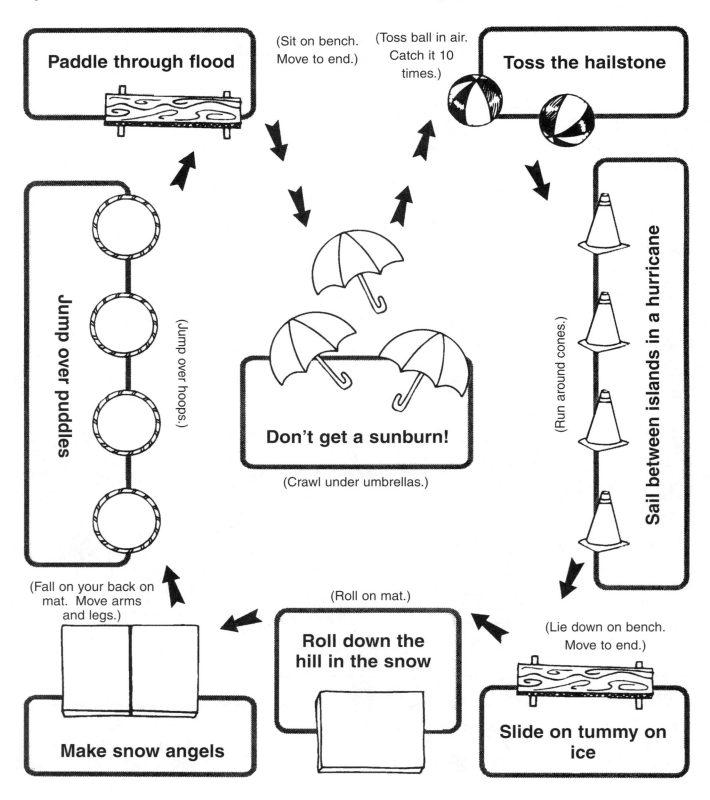

**Paddle through flood**

(Sit on bench. Move to end.)

(Toss ball in air. Catch it 10 times.)

**Toss the hailstone**

**Jump over puddles**

(Jump over hoops.)

**Sail between islands in a hurricane**

(Run around cones.)

**Don't get a sunburn!**

(Crawl under umbrellas.)

(Fall on your back on mat. Move arms and legs.)

(Roll on mat.)

(Lie down on bench. Move to end.)

**Roll down the hill in the snow**

**Make snow angels**

**Slide on tummy on ice**

# Be Weather Wizards

Help children learn to observe, record, and predict the weather by following the steps below.

**Step One:** Set the Stage

1. Read *I Can Be a Weather Forecaster* by Claire Martin and/or *Weather Forecasting* by Gail Gibbons.

2. Visit a weather station, if possible.

**Step Two:** Build Weather Stations

1. Organize the children into small cooperative groups.

2. Challenge them to set up their own weather stations using weather instruments, including the ones they have made during the unit. Have each group use page 65 to plan the use of the weather station.

3. Encourage cooperative problem-solving.

4. Help each group find a safe place for their weather station.

**Step Three:** Observe, Record, and Predict the Weather

Use the Weather Wizard Data Collection worksheets on pages 68 and 69 with the activities in Step Three.

1. Teach students how to "read" their instruments and record their observations and findings.

2. Provide frequent opportunities to observe and record weather conditions and readings on weather instruments during a designated period of time (such as a week).

3. Help students use their observations and recordings to predict the weather. Use "Weather Wizard Secrets" (page 66), "What's That Cloud?" (page 67), and other knowledge gained during the unit to help make the predictions.

4. Encourage students to evaluate their work by comparing their predictions to professional predictions and actual weather.

# Be Weather Wizards *(cont.)*

**Step Four:** Prepare Weather Reports

1. Assist groups in using their weather records, observations, and predictions to prepare visual aids (see weather map, pages 48–49) and scripts for weather reports. Have them read and listen to professional weather reports in newspapers, on radio, and on TV so that they get a feel for the content of these reports. (An excellent resource is The Weather Channel.) This may be assigned as a homework activity. Encourage students to bring in newspaper pages, audio, and/or videotaped recordings of weather reports. Be sure that they notice that most reports consist of two parts: a) reporting the current and just-past weather and b) forecasting the weather to come.

2. Arrange for a variety of media by which the children may share their reports:

   • a large display area such as a bulletin board
   • a pretend radio or TV broadcast
   • a space in the class or school newspaper

3. Let each group choose the medium which it will use to share its report. Ensure that each team has an opportunity to share and that each team member participates in the preparation of the report.

4. After the report has been shared, encourage the children to evaluate their work.

**Step Five:** Share Beyond the Classroom

Choose one or more of the following ways to share the weather reports with others.

1. Arrange to have your class prepare a display that will be placed where everyone in the school can see it—for example, on a bulletin board by the office.

2. Ask for a short time each day for a week when your class can "broadcast" its reports to the school on the public address system.

3. Arrange for the audio or video recording (upper-grade students can often help with this) of student-produced "radio" and "TV" weather reports. Play these at a Parents' Night, in the school cafeteria during lunch, for other classrooms, etc.

4. Write your local newspaper and explain what your class is doing. Enclose photographs (a high school photography class may like to take these pictures). Your students will love being in the paper.

5. Invite a local weather forecaster to visit your classroom so that students can exchange information with him.

# Build a Weather Station

In a small group, set up a weather station using the weather instruments you have made. Each group member should contribute one instrument.

| Things to Decide |
|---|

1. What will we study? Who will be responsible?

   We will study _____.

   _____ will be responsible for

   _____.

   _____will be responsible for

   _____.

   _____will be responsible for

   _____.

   _____ will be responsible for

   _____.

   _____ will be responsible for

   _____.

2. What do we need in our weather station? _____

   _____

   _____

3. Where will our weather station be located? (Your teacher will help you find a safe, open, flat, and convenient place.) _____

   _____

4. Make a sign for your weather station.

   Name it and list the people in your group.

# Weather Wizard Secrets

**Predict nice weather if:**

- Wind is from the west or southwest.

- You see cirrus, cirrocumulus, or cirrostratus clouds.

- Cumulus clouds are separate and disappearing.

**Predict bad weather if:**

- Wind is from the south or southeast (or from the east in winter).

- You see low clouds such as stratus or nimbostratus.

- Cumulus clouds are getting bigger.

- Halo rings are around the moon.

**Predict cloudy weather if:**

- You see low stratocumulus clouds.

# What's That Cloud?

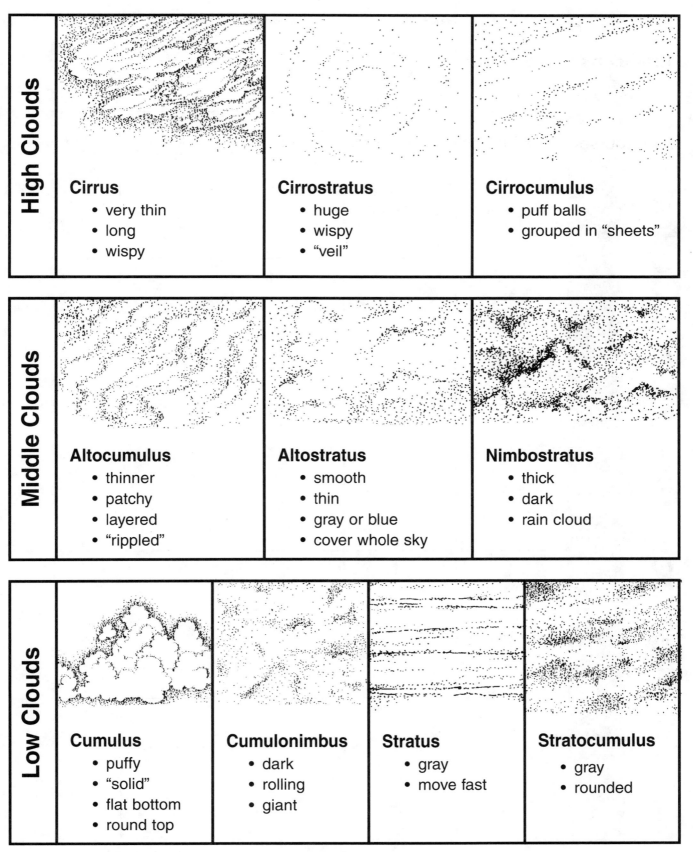

**High Clouds**

**Cirrus**
- very thin
- long
- wispy

**Cirrostratus**
- huge
- wispy
- "veil"

**Cirrocumulus**
- puff balls
- grouped in "sheets"

**Middle Clouds**

**Altocumulus**
- thinner
- patchy
- layered
- "rippled"

**Altostratus**
- smooth
- thin
- gray or blue
- cover whole sky

**Nimbostratus**
- thick
- dark
- rain cloud

**Low Clouds**

**Cumulus**
- puffy
- "solid"
- flat bottom
- round top

**Cumulonimbus**
- dark
- rolling
- giant

**Stratus**
- gray
- move fast

**Stratocumulus**
- gray
- rounded

**Attach to page 69 here.**

# Weather Wizard Data Collection

| Date | Temperature | | Air Pressure | Precipitation | Clouds |
|------|-----|-----|---|---|---|
| | AM | PM | | | |
| | | | | | |
| | | | | | |
| | | | | | |
| | | | | | |

# Weather Wizard Data Collection (cont.)

| Wind | | My Forecast | Newspaper, Radio, or TV Forecast | Actual Weather |
|---|---|---|---|---|
| Speed | Direction | | | |
| | | | | |
| | | | | |
| | | | | |
| | | | | |

**Attach to page 68 here.**

# Technology Extenders

The following activities may be used as conventional culminating projects or as technology extenders to reinforce the content learning of this unit with computer experience. Each activity is designed to involve students in merging technology and the subject matter of the thematic unit.

1. **Temperature Log, Graph, and Reflection**

   *Software:* any word-processing and spreadsheet program such as *ClarisWorks*, etc.

   *Activity:* Create a template of cells to record the high temperature each day for one week on a spreadsheet. Print it out and give one to each student to log their observations. Show them how to record their logs on the computer. Then show them how to use the computer to convert their spreadsheet records to a graph. Have them compose one summary or "reflection" sentence explaining what happened that week, and write that at the bottom of the graph. Save and print out each student's record to post on the board.

2. **Weather Newsletter**

   *Software:* any word-processing program such as *Word, Word Perfect,* etc.

   *Activity:* Create a one-page newsletter layout as a template. Print out a blank copy for each student. After they have filled the page with their drawings, observations, questions, and facts, help them to enter their work on the computer and print out the final copy to exchange with the class. (You might wish to have each student select one weather fact from page 29 to use.)

3. **Weather Pie Graph and Reflection**

   *Software:* any word-processing and spreadsheet program.

   *Activity:* Help students set up a piece of paper divided into quarters labeled "Sunny," "Rainy," "Snowy," and "Cloudy," respectively. Have students tally the days for one month, according to the weather. Show them how to record this on a spreadsheet on the computer and then use the spreadsheet program to automatically convert the data into a pie graph. Save and print in color for the bulletin board, with copies for each student to take home with tally sheet and spreadsheet.

4. **Fall Turns to Winter**

   *Software: Kid Pix 2* or any paint, draw, and graphics program.

   *Activity:* Help students learn to use the drawing, brush, paint can, and rubber stamp tools to draw a picture of bare trees, leaves on the ground, and snow falling. Complete the picture by adding a line of text like "Winter Comes After Fall." Save, print, and post these on the board or collect as a slide show for Parent's Night.

5. **Talking Weather Days**

   *Software: Kid Pix 2* or any paint, draw, and graphics program.

   *Activity:* After discussing favorite activities on rainy, sunny, cloudy, and snowy days, help students use paint can, brush, line, and rubber stamp tools to draw pictures of their favorite activities for each day. Afterward, use the computer microphone to record their narrations and descriptions for each picture. Save and collect as a "slide show" for Parents' Night.

6. **A Book of Clouds**

   *Software: Kid Pix 2* or any paint, draw, and graphics program.

   Activity: After reviewing *cirrus, stratus,* and *cumulus* clouds, help students to draw pictures of each type of cloud on the computer, using the paint, draw, and graphics program. Use a separate page for each cloud, add blue and white for sky and cloud colors, and label each cloud as a page heading. Design a cover page titled "My Book of Clouds." Print out each student's four pages and have them staple the pages together as a booklet to display.

# Weather Bulletin Board

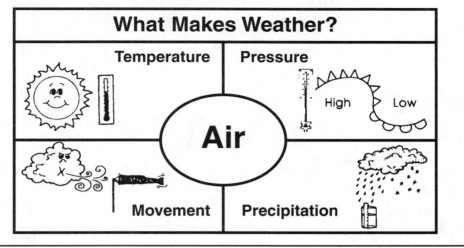

## Objectives

This bulletin board is designed to teach and reinforce the four components of weather. It can also be used to display and teach the instruments used to measure each weather component (see Extension below).

**Materials:** butcher paper and/or colored construction paper; scissors; stapler; pushpins

**Optional:** foil; cotton batting; silver glitter; thick craft yarn; narrow red ribbon

## Construction

Reproduce patterns (pages 72–78) onto appropriately-colored construction paper; highlight with crayons or markers; and cut out. **Optional:** Make raindrops from foil; add glitter to snowflakes; cut clouds from cotton batting; use red ribbon for thermometer and barometer fluid; use yarn for the wind's breath.

Cover background of bulletin board with blue butcher paper. Use construction paper strips or yarn to divide bulletin board as shown in the diagram above. Add title, words, and patterns as shown in the diagram, or use as described below.

**Directions:** By building it gradually during the weather unit, this bulletin board can be used as a teaching tool.

Start with only the title and divisions in place. Have the children brainstorm answers to the title question, "What Makes Weather?" Record their answers on a chart for reference during the unit.

Continue by asking, "Where does weather happen?" Lead the discussion to conclude that weather takes place in the air and add that word to the display.

Complete the bulletin board as concepts and vocabulary are introduced during successive lessons.

## Extension

The weather instruments that measure each weather component may be added to each section. Patterns are on pages 76–78.

# Bulletin Board Patterns

**Sun**

72

# Bulletin Board Patterns *(cont.)*

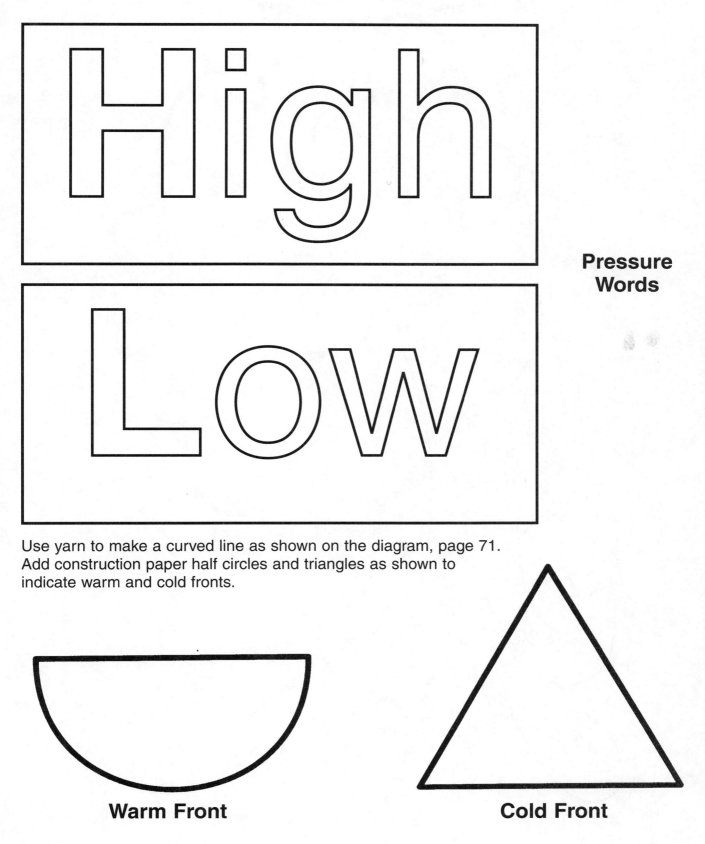

**Pressure Words**

Use yarn to make a curved line as shown on the diagram, page 71. Add construction paper half circles and triangles as shown to indicate warm and cold fronts.

**Warm Front**

**Cold Front**

# Bulletin Board Patterns *(cont.)*

**Wind**

74

# Bulletin Board Patterns *(cont.)*

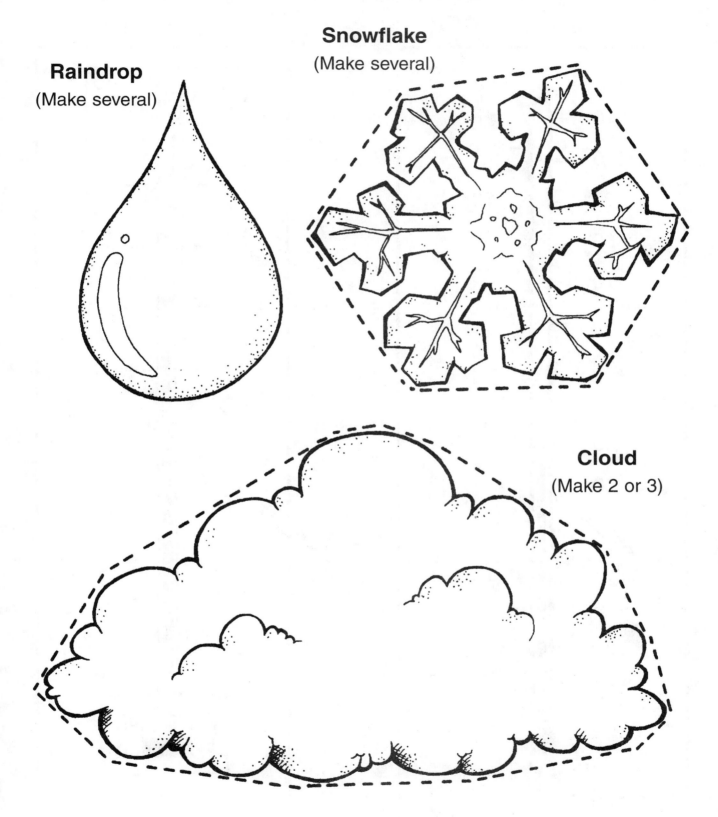

**Raindrop**
(Make several)

**Snowflake**
(Make several)

**Cloud**
(Make 2 or 3)

# Bulletin Board Patterns *(cont.)*

### Thermometer

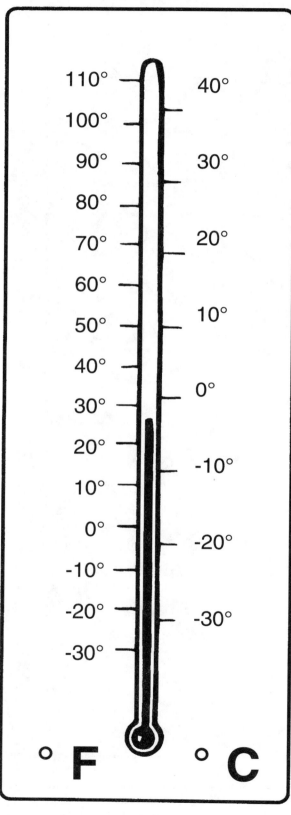

### Barometer

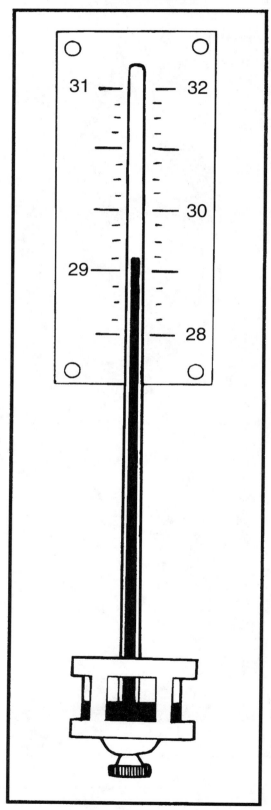

76

# Bulletin Board Patterns *(cont.)*

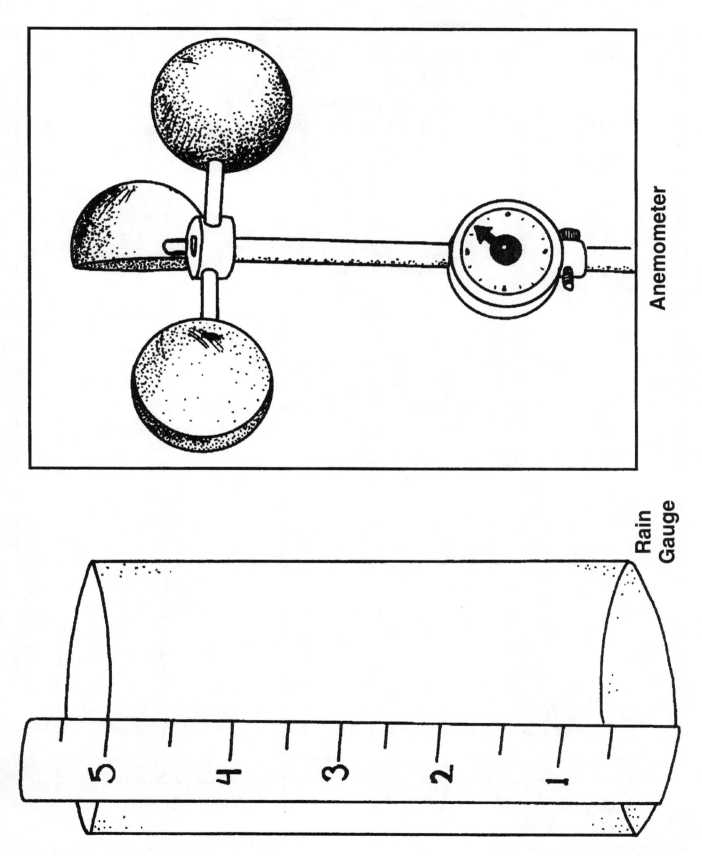

**Anemometer**

**Rain Gauge**

# Bulletin Board Patterns *(cont.)*

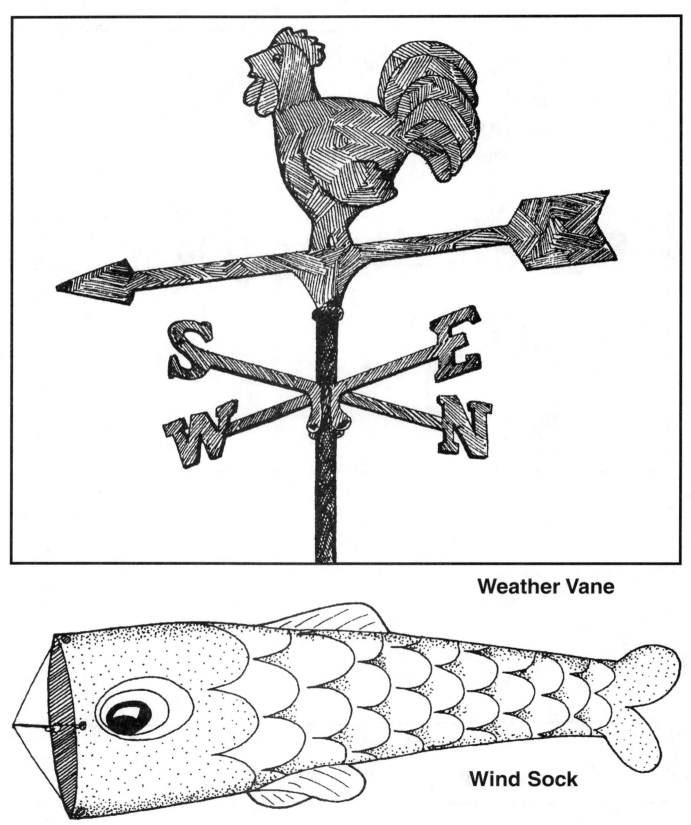

**Weather Vane**

**Wind Sock**

# Answer Key

**p. 18**

1. little drops of water or ice hanging in the atmosphere

2. cirrus, cumulus, stratus (in any order);
   a. cirrus, b. cumulus, c. stratus

3. cirrus

4. cumulus

5. stratus

6. a cloud made of water droplets formed at ground level

**p. 19**

1. cumulus

2. rain

3. If there are fluffy clouds in the morning, by evening it will rain.

4. Accept reasonable answers.

5. droppin'; head; fountains; way; sails

**p. 27**

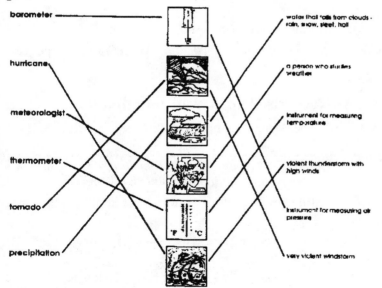

barometer — water that falls from clouds - rain, snow, sleet, hail

hurricane — a person who studies weather

meteorologist — instrument for measuring temperature

thermometer — violent thunderstorm with high winds

tornado — instrument for measuring air pressure

precipitation — very violent windstorm

**p. 30**

Possible answers include: bus; bum; club; cub; in; mob; nimbus; no; numb; on; sum; son; sub; sun; us

**p. 31**

A. Answers may vary. See *The Cloud Book* index.

B. altostratus
   cirrocumulus
   cirrus
   cumulus
   fog
   nimbostratus
   stratus

(These are just a few. Students may wish to include some of the colloquial terms for clouds, as well.)

**p. 46**

1. Washington, Oregon, Idaho

2. Montana, Wyoming, Utah, Colorado

3. California, Nevada

4. Arizona, New Mexico

# Bibliography

## Suggested Books

Barrett, Judi. *Cloudy with a Chance of Meatballs.* Aladdin Books, 1978

Bauer, Caroline Feller. *Midnight Snowman.* Atheneum, 1987

Belanger, Claude. *I Like the Rain.* Rigby. (Available as Big Book or little book with accompanying tape. Order from Rigby, P.O. Box 797, Crystal Lake, IL 60014. (800) 822-8661)

Branley, Franklyn M. *Flash, Crash, Rumble and Roll.* Thomas Y. Crowell, 1985

Branley, Franklyn M. *Rain and Hail.* Thomas Y. Crowell, 1983

Butler, Beverly. *The Wind and Me.* Dodd, Mead & Co., 1971

dePaola, Tomie. *The Cloud Book.* Holiday House, 1975

Davis, Hubert. *A January Fog Will Freeze a Hog and Other Weather Folklore.* Crown Pub., 1977

Ets, Marie Hall. *Gilberto and the Wind.* Viking Press, 1963

Euvremer, Teryl. *Sun's Up.* Crown Publishers, Inc., 1987

Freeman, Don. *A Rainbow of My Own.* Viking Press, 1966

Garelick, May. *Where Does the Butterfly Go When It Rains?* Young, Scott Books, 1961

Gibbons, Gail. *Weather Forecasting.* Macmillan, 1987

Hoff, Syd. *When Will It Snow?* Harper & Row, 1971

Hutchins, Pat. *The Wind Blew.* Macmillan Pub. Co., 1974

Kalan, Robert. *Rain.* Greenwillow Books, 1978

Keats, Ezra Jack. *The Snowy Day.* Viking, 1981

Kuskin, Karla. *James and the Rain.* Harper & Row, 1957

Martin, Claire. *I Can Be a Weather Forecaster.* Children's Press, 1987

McCully, Emily Arnold. *First Snow.* Harper & Row, 1985

McKie, Roy & Eastman, P.D. *Snow.* Beginner Books, Random House, 1962

Moncure, Jane Belk. *What Causes It? A Beginning Book About Weather.* Children's Press, 1977

Morgan, Allen. *Sadie and the Snowman.* Kids Can Press, 1985

Munsch, Robert. *Millicent and the Wind.* Firefly Books Ltd., 1984

An Ontario Science Center Book of Experiments. *Science Works,* Kids Can Press, 1984

Pyk, Ann. *The Hammer of Thunder.* G.P. Putnam's Sons, 1972

Shulevitz, Uri. *Rain Rain Rivers.* Farrar Straus & Giroux, 1969

Smith, Henry. *Amazing Air.* Methuen Children's Books, Ltd., 1982

Stoutenburg, Adrien. *American Tall Tales.* Penguin, 1976

Suzuki, David. *Looking at Weather.* New Data Enterprises, 1988

Tresselt, Alvin. *Hide and Seek Fog.* Lothrop, Lee & Shepard, 1988

Tressalt, Alvin. *Rain Drop Splash.* Lothrop, Lee & Shepard, 1946

Webster, Vera. *Weather Experiments (A New True Book).* Children's Press, 1982

Wheeler, Cindy. *Marmalade's Snowy Day.* Alfred A. Knopf, 1982

Wyatt, Valerie. *Weather Watch.* Addison-Wesley, 1990

Yashima, Taro. *Umbrella.* The Viking Press, 1967

Zolotow, Charlotte. *When the Wind Stops.* Harper & Row, 1975

## Records, Tapes, and Songbooks

Coyne, Debbie (compiled by), *Everybody Sings* (DMC Publications, 1991)

Glazer, Tom (compiled by), *Tom Glazer's Treasury of Songs for Children* (Doubleday, 1964)

Raffi. *Rise and Shine* "Ducks Like Rain" Troubadour Records Ltd., 1982

Raffi. *Singable Songs* "Mr. Sun." Troubadour Records Ltd., 1976

Rosenshontz. *Share It!* "Eat It Up!" Kids' Records, 1982

Youngheart Records. *We All Live Together Vol. 2.* "The World Is A Rainbow," "The Freeze." 1978

## Poetry

de Regniers, B.S. (selected by). *Sing a Song of Popcorn.* "Mostly Weather" section. Scholastic, 1988.